DO NOT REMOVE
CARDS FROM POCKET

This address, dealing with the history of The Cheyenne Airport and The Wyoming Aviation Hall of Fame was delivered at a "1995 Wyoming Meeting" of The Newcomen Society of the United States held in Cheyenne, when Captain "Billy" Walker, Jr. was guest of honor and speaker on August 11th, 1995.

Wyoming Aviation
Hall of Fame

Captain Harold "Slim" Lewis

Captain Ralph S. Johnson

Major W. Dillard "Pic" Walker
General Samuel C. Phillips

The Cheyenne Airport

and

The Wyoming Aviation

Hall of Fame

CAPTAIN WILLIAM D. "BILLY" WALKER, JR.

With Contributions by The Cheyenne Airport Board

and

The Cheyenne Corral of the Westerners

THE NEWCOMEN SOCIETY OF THE UNITED STATES

NEW YORK   EXTON   PRINCETON   PORTLAND

1996

Newcomen Publication Number 1463

❦

Copyright, 1995
CHEYENNE AIRPORT
AND THE WYOMING
AVIATION HALL OF
FAME

❦

*Permission to abstract is granted
provided proper credit is allowed*

❦

*The Newcomen Society, as a body,
is not responsible for opinions
expressed in the following pages*

❦

First Printing: January, 1996

 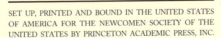

SET UP, PRINTED AND BOUND IN THE UNITED STATES
OF AMERICA FOR THE NEWCOMEN SOCIETY OF THE
UNITED STATES BY PRINCETON ACADEMIC PRESS, INC.

Newcomen Society Members and Guests, Ladies and Gentlemen:

W E THANK THE NEWCOMEN SOCIETY OF THE UNITED STATES for honoring Cheyenne and the State of Wyoming again. Tonight we celebrate the 75th anniversary of the Cheyenne Airport and the initiation of the Wyoming Aviation Hall of Fame. Sixty years ago, Cheyenne was the major western stop between Chicago and the west coast for United Air Lines. United established a major maintenance depot here, as well as a stewardess training school which graduated over 80,000 young women. Two of its chief test pilots, Ralph Johnson and "Slim" Lewis, were stationed here. Chairman Jack Hughes invited United Air Lines to participate in tonight's program, but they refused his invitation. The company seems to have forgotten that Cheyenne, and not Denver, was once their major hub in the Rocky Mountain States.

We honor tonight four great men who pioneered aviation in Wyoming and the west. In addition to Ralph Johnson and Slim Lewis, we honor General Sam Phillips, a Cheyenne native, who became a four-star General as head of the Apollo Space Program at its peak in 1969, and Major W. Dillard "Pic" Walker, who taught over 5,000 pilots to fly during World War II and was instrumental in the initial development of the Civil Air Patrol in Wyoming and the west.

It is my pleasure to introduce Billy Walker, the son of Pic Walker, to tell you about the ventures of his father and the other three inductees. My friend, Ralph Johnson, is here tonight and he will be given an opportunity to speak for himself.

Billy Walker grew up in Cheyenne and Saratoga. He learned to fly here under the tutelage of his father, Ralph Johnson, Marvin Stevenson, and other pioneer aviators. At the age of 14, Billy couldn't wait to try his wings and absconded with his father's Cessna 180 to take a couple of friends for a flight in the Saratoga area. Billy didn't tell his dad about this until he approached his 30th birthday.

Billy Walker is a great pilot in his own right. In 1967, he joined Frontier Airlines as a DC-3 co-pilot. He stayed with Frontier for 23 years, ending up as a Captain on the MD-80 and the chief spokesman for the pilots. He even remained as custodial representative of Frontier through its bankruptcy proceedings. Billy is now with the America West Air Line where he remains as a check pilot and instructor on the ultra modern Airbus - A-320, fly-by-wire aircraft.

I present to you Billy Walker.

JACK HUGHES, CHAIRMAN OF THE WYOMING COMMITTEE IN NEWCOMEN PRESENTS THE NEWCOMEN AWARD TO BILLY WALKER

THE AIR HALL OF FAME (WITH THE NEW-COMEN AWARD PROMINENTLY SHOWN) IS ON PERMANENT DISPLAY IN THE LOBBY OF THE CHEYENNE AIRPORT

Members of The Newcomen Society, good evening; a hearty welcome, as well, to those of you who are guests.

TONIGHT WE ARE GOING TO CELEBRATE the rich history of the Cheyenne Airport and some of the fine pioneer airmen who helped to make aviation what it is today.

I am humbled by Governor Hathaway's introduction. Thank you very much, Governor. Ladies and Gentlemen, it is a distinct pleasure to speak to you tonight, here in the shadow of Cheyenne's historic airfield. I am grateful to be a part of this evening's program and am doubly honored, as we are going to pay tribute to four aviation stalwarts, one of whom was my father and another, my mentor. They were Cheyomingites who played such a big part in the tremendous success of the aviation industry.

The last time I was asked to speak I thought my talk was going along O.K., when I noticed a big fellow, sitting in the front row, was carrying a huge 357 magnum. Seeing that weapon made me a little nervous. Then he pulls out this enormous gun and sits it up on the table in front of him, and I became real nervous and started stuttering and stammering and my speech started going poorly. I guess he noticed my nervousness and passed a note up to me. The note said: "Captain, I ain't goin' to shoot ya, but I shore would appreciate your pointing out the guy that asked you to speak." So, Mr. Hughes and Mr. Kelso, you might want to sit a bit lower in your seats tonight!

As a youngster growing up in Cheyenne, I naturally assumed that the Wright Brothers, Lindbergh, Rickenbacker, and all famous aviators were from Cheyenne. This somewhat inaccurate view was the result of being born into a Cheyenne aviation family. My father (a pioneer airman, took his first flight in 1924); my mother, (the first female to learn to fly in Wyoming), and my parents' closest friends, The Johnsons, were among a number of people who created my world as a small child. That world centered around the Cheyenne airport. Since then, I have never wished

to be anything other than a pilot and, happily, for over 30 years, I have been paid for just doing my hobby. Luck does play a part in the scheme of things!

Back in 1903, a couple of significant events occurred. Orville and Wilbur Wright successfully flew their flimsy aircraft from Kill Devil Hills, near Kitty Hawk, North Carolina, and the State of Wyoming hung Tom Horn. There were times, perhaps, that some of the early aviation people around here might have wished that the Wright's had been hung instead of poor ol' Tom... For sure, aviation's maturation has not been effortless.

Significantly, the hanging of Tom Horn sort of ushered out the wild and wooly West, while the Wright's first flight ushered in a new era of technological advancement, the likes of which the world had never seen.

Cheyenne would become a major player in the phenomenal growth of aviation. Some of its citizens would distinguish themselves by their innovations and inventions, and, thereby, bring credit to the community. Sometimes, things would happen serendipitously as well. So, luck played a part too. Someone once said, if there is a choice between luck and skill...take luck!

Cheyenne has been a big part of our country's growth since 1867. Cheyenne survived the days of buffalo hunters and Indian fighters, when many communities sprung up around the country only to become ghost towns a few years later. While the state capital city has never supported a large population, few cities have enjoyed the world's admiration and respect as much as Cheyenne, a place noted for its progressive ways along with Frontier Days, the Union Pacific Railroad, and women's rights (championed by Wyoming and included the Women's Equal Suffrage Act of 1869).

The first time the aviation world touched Cheyenne was in 1911 at the fairgrounds and it was not an impressive beginning. The warm temperature and the 6,300 feet altitude made Charles Walsh's performance, in his diaphanous ship, somewhat of a disappointment to the spectators.

Not much happened around here with aircraft until after WWI when the U.S. Post Office gave birth to commercial aviation with the start of the airmail routes.

THE FIRST AIRMAIL FLIGHT FROM CHEYENNE WAS FLOWN BY BUCK HEFFRON IN A
LIBERTY POWERED DEHAVILLAND DH-4 WITH A DESTINATION OF SALT LAKE CITY.

Recognizing an opportunity, Cheyenne's civic leaders lobbied hard to
be one of the airmail's cross country sites. It was an uphill fight, too. Not
only did Cheyenne not have an airport, there was little money to finance
the development of one. The character of our Cheyenne forefathers still
shines today. The folks here were not going to let a golden opportunity
slip through their grasp. They did what they had to do to get things going
with the hope the Post Office would eventually reimburse the initial
development costs. Ultimately, Congress did reimburse these costs.
Cheyenne's success in securing a site would become Denver's envy until
aircraft, developed way in the future, allowed flight over the high
mountain peaks.

Airmail brought commercial aviation to Cheyenne in 1920 and a local
man, by the name of Hollister, brought to Cheyenne a Curtiss Oriole
biplane giving birth to general aviation that same year. The Oriole, flown
by WWI pilot C. A. McKenzie, carried aloft Cheyenne's first passenger,
a lady barber by the name of Elizabeth Brown.

The first airmail flight from Cheyenne was flown by Buck Heffron in
a Liberty powered DeHavilland DH-4 with a destination of Salt Lake
City. Jimmy Murray brought the first load of mail into Cheyenne
September 9, 1920. A couple of months later, he crashed into Medicine
Bow peak west of Laramie. He and the mail survived; the DH-4 did not.
There were many accidents with fatalities, too. These aircraft were barely
suitable for the mountains of the Rocky Mountain West. They had a

range of 300 miles and a payload of 500 pounds. They flew 110 mph at a ceiling of 10,000 feet, (barely enough to clear the mountain passes), but they were the best aircraft available back then.

In 1921 famed WWI Ace, Eddie Rickenbacker, crashed during a night landing in Cheyenne while on a west-to-east speed record attempt. His pride and the aircraft were the only things damaged. Back in 1921, oil drums and farmers' bonfires were the night navigation system. This, of course, was not feasible on a regular basis. Initially, mail was transferred to the railway for night movement and then transferred back to another aircraft during daylight. The Lincoln Highway as well as familiar landmarks and the good ol' Union Pacific railroad, were used for daytime navigation. My Dad used to joke that navigating via the railroad worked out pretty good...until someone left a switch open.

By 1923, lighted beacons became common for night navigation. These were located at emergency landing fields every 25-35 miles along the mail route. By 1924, night flying became a regular part of the program. Interestingly, a few beacons remained in use into the 1970's. In fact, the last one (from Corona Pass west of Boulder) now sits in my uncle Gib's ol' hangar in Granby, Colorado.

Airmail flying was considered experimental until the Kelly Airmail Act of 1925 provided for the transfer of the mail routes to private carriers. The Air Mail Service was finally discontinued after everything was transferred to the private carriers by mid 1927. The early airmail flying was an exciting time for the Cheyenne residents, while it lasted.

Undaunted, Cheyenne's progressive spirit took hold and the citizens began looking forward to hosting the emerging airlines. Lawrence Murray and Vern Gersmehl, two of the airmail people, stayed in Cheyenne. One of the WWI pilots who flew the mail out of Cheyenne, Slim Lewis, returned to Cheyenne as Boeing Air Transport's chief pilot.

Time prevents mentioning the names of all the individuals (pilots & ground crew) who made contributions, but there were a few, like Lewis, who earned their rightful place in aviation history.

Harold T. "Slim" Lewis began life in 1894 and became an "Early Bird" by soloing an old Curtiss Pusher in 1916. He became an instructor and early test pilot in 1918 and was flying the mail for the Post Office, following WWI. Three of his runs were Omaha-Cheyenne and Chey-

BOEING B-29

enne-Salt Lake and Salt Lake-San Francisco. Then, in 1927, he became Chief Pilot for Boeing Air Transport and was based in Cheyenne. Following the merger, Lewis stayed with United and was in charge of the western region. In 1937, he left United to help start Trans Canada Airlines. Two years later, Lewis was back at Boeing as chief pilot doing what he loved most—test flying. By then, WWII was on the door step and more than 6,000 B-17's and 1,000 B-29's needed to be test flown. Lewis flew many flights personally, as many as six flights a day.

When the war ended, Boeing laid off more than 60,000 employees in one day! Lewis, however, stayed on another year flight testing the "Stratocruiser," a big four-engine commercial airliner that United flew

CAPTAIN HAROLD "SLIM" LEWIS

for several years. But, this was dull stuff for a man who had flown the mail across Wyoming. Lewis felt the calling of nature and retired to his cattle ranch north of Cheyenne until he folded his wings in 1965.

Another local pilot, Jack Knight, became legendary with the first transcontinental all-night airmail flight in 1921. He was a pilot with United Airlines when he died in Cheyenne in 1945. A side note to this is that Knight was a friend of my father and Ralph Johnson. Through Dad and Ralph, I ended up with the leather jacket Knight wore the night of his famous flight. I gave it to Frontier Airlines and we presented it to the North Platte, Nebraska Airport Authority. It is now in a prominent display at the terminal in North Platte where he began his celebrated flight. I sort of wish I had kept it for this evening.

Pilots like Lewis and Knight were special. More than once they had occasion to buzz a ranch to warn the sleeping inhabitants of a barn on fire. Occasionally they would drop candy in little hand-made parachutes to the isolated ranch children.

In addition to winning the airmail contract, Boeing Air Transport Company established its main overhaul base at Cheyenne, growing from an initial 75 men to over 500 within a short period of time.

In May of 1927, Charles A. Lindbergh electrified the world with his non-stop flight from New York to Paris. Almost single-handedly, Lindbergh started a tremendous boom to the commercial aircraft industry. People were no longer skeptical to the feasibility of air travel. America became enthusiastic about flying, seemingly overnight. A few months later, Lindbergh stopped in Cheyenne with his plane "The Spirit of Saint Louis." Cheyenne was always a friendly place to a weary traveler and gave an especially warm welcome to America's newest hero.

In 1927, Boeing built 25 Model B-40 Wasp powered aircraft with over three times the payload of the DH-4. The Wasp would prove much more reliable than the old WWI Liberty's and OX-5 engines. The speed was still around 110 MPH, topping out at 119 MPH. The 40B, as it became known, offered several improvements. It still was an open-cockpit bi-plane. However, it featured an enclosed cabin for passengers and took just 32 hours to fly coast-to-coast, whereas just 15 years before the "Vin Fizz" took 49 days.

During this same period, Western Air Express (now a part of Delta) was awarded the Cheyenne-Denver-Pueblo mail contract and flew 430 passengers in and out of Cheyenne the first year. Commercial air travel was coming of age. Now, that many can travel at one time on a Boeing 747.

1929 saw some improvement in aircraft development with the Boeing Model 80A, a tri-engine Hornet powered two-pilot ship that more than doubled the payload of the Model 40B. One fascinating aspect of the Model 80 was that the second model, the 80B, was an open cockpit rather than the enclosed cockpit of the 80A. Apparently, some of the old WWI pilots objected to being inside. They were used to the sights and sounds of the flying wires and engine noise and, being pilots, were resistant to change. Eventually, the newer practicalities overruled the force of old habits.

The 80A was used by Boeing Air Transport and our intrepid friend, Jepp Jepppesen, was flying one through Cheyenne the first time Ralph Johnson met him in 1932. At that time Ralph was an army pilot flying General Wynans around the country in a tri-motored Fokker F-3 and had a stop-over at Ft. D.A. Russell, near Cheyenne. For those of you that were not buffalo hunters or Indian fighters, Ft. D. A. Russell is now known as Francis E. Warren A.F.B.

While many things were being done to improve aviation throughout the world, things at Cheyenne were progressing, too. By 1930, Boeing Air Transport had become part of United Air Transport Company through a series of mergers with other fledgling airlines. By 1934, they were fully merged and operating under one livery.

Early in 1930, some executives had been talking about placing stewards aboard the 80A's, but nothing much happened until Ellen Church, a diminutive San Francisco nurse, proposed the idea and a new profession was born. Later, a stewardess training school was established in Cheyenne and 83,000 young women were trained here.

Jepp's lovely wife, Nadine, was a stewardess on the old 80A until Jepp convinced her to be his partner in life. By then he was producing his "little black book" (not that kind of little-black-book). Jepp's "Little Black Book" was his detailing of each airport so that he would have reminders of hazards, topography, runways and facilities, etc. Other pilots became aware of this and, in short order, he had a growing cottage industry in his Cheyenne basement. Now the entire World knows of Jepp and what he and Nadine have done to improve air travel. The new terminal at Denver International Airport is appropriately named for Jepp and he was recently inducted into the Aviation Hall of Fame in Dayton, Ohio. I have enjoyed my association with Jepp for many years as a fellow member of "Quiet Birdmen."

The Cheyenne stewardess school was running full tilt when I was learning to fly and I must admit that, at that time, I considered that school as our nation's richest natural resource. Sadly, in 1961, the school was closed and moved to Denver and later to Chicago. Wouldn't you know it...I, a bachelor then, moved back to Cheyenne in 1964, a few short years after its closure.

BOEING 40-B

ELREY "JEPP" JEPPESEN
THIS STATUE OF JEPP IS ON PERMANENT
DISPLAY AT THE DENVER INTERNATIONAL
AIRPORT.

BOEING 80-A

Meanwhile, back in the 1930's—other things were happening around here. The Weather Service moved from downtown, where it had been since the 1870's to the airport. In those days, weather was a very serious matter when your aircraft lacked the performance to fly over it. So, it was nice to receive a personal briefing from the friendly weather man. With automation, this system has all but been lost, but we still prefer to have the personal briefing.

Radio navigational aids were being perfected and installed to help pilots get around Sherman Hill and Elk Mountain. These helped, although they were not totally successful, as crashes continued all too often. The old beacon installed at Ft. D.A. Russell provided a fix for the east-west runway and proved a boon to the safety of all weather flights in and out of Cheyenne. I remember using this in the 1950's before it was replaced by the OMNI station.

In 1930, Boeing developed the Model 247 and United bought every one of them. Initially, this caused a problem for the other airlines. For a while United had the best ship available for passenger transportation. The 247 was a low-wing twin-engine all-metal retractable gear aircraft that weighed 16,000 pounds carrying 10 passengers at 160 MPH, cutting the coast-to-coast time to 27-1/2 hours. United began operating these aircraft out of Cheyenne in 1933.

By 1935, United was increasing its schedule to keep up the demand created by more public acceptance of air travel. This was largely due to the development of the Douglas DC-3. The venerable DC-3, still in use around the world today, was a real step up in safety and passenger comfort.

Things were improving until 1934 when politics did as they are apparently designed to do—muck up the works!

FDR canceled the airmail contracts and ordered the Army to fly the mail. This was a foreseeable disaster that lasted 75 days and cost the lives of a dozen Army pilots to crashes. Two (Lt. A. R. Kerwin and Lt. F. L. Howard) were lost at Cheyenne. Lost because the army aircraft were totally unsuitable for the job. Men like Ralph Johnson and Jepp Jepppesen knew this as they had flown the same type of aircraft previously and knew the Army boys were being short changed in the safety department.

It took these accidents to wake ol' FDR up and give the contracts back to the airlines. Even with the return of the contracts, politics slapped fairness out of the way and several airlines lost some of their previous routes to others. Chicago to Dallas, for example, had belonged to United. After the restructuring, it was given away to the Braniff brothers.

By 1935 there were three airlines operating out of Cheyenne. Everett Hogan flew the inaugural flight, as Wyoming Air Service began a north-south route. With Western and United having begun earlier, Cheyenne enjoyed having arrivals and departures going in four directions.

United bought the Cheyenne to Denver route from Wyoming Air Service in 1937. Wyoming Air Service later became Inland Air Lines and in 1944 merged with Western. A few years ago Western merged again and became part of Delta. My uncle, Lee Osborn, flew for Inland out of Cheyenne in Boeing 247's and eventually retired in 1966 as senior Western captain.

From these pre-WWII years, Cheyenne kept pace with the rest of the world in air transportation. But now things were to become hectic with the US of A being pulled into the war. United's maintenance and overhaul base continued to operate and United added a modification center located on the north side of the airport. "Green" aircraft were flown from the factory to Cheyenne for the addition of all the operational equipment, latest modifications, and specialty items. Then they were test flown before turning them over to the combat crews. The maintenance base grew to over 3,000 employees working in three shifts around the clock. It was a far cry from the original 75 employees back in 1921.

During this time, Captain Ralph S. Johnson flew over 7000 test flights from the Cheyenne airport. He had joined United as a "mate", flying the Ford Tri-motor. In 1934 he became a captain, and in 1935 he was sent to Cheyenne as the Chief Test Pilot and Research Engineer. Between 1935 and 1947, he was a very busy fellow. He must have become used to being busy because he became even busier after he "retired" in 1947. Surprisingly, many of Ralph's accomplishments occurred after United pulled out of Cheyenne.

There were three phases to Johnson's storied career—military, airlines and general aviation. Johnson's proclivity to improving things and making aviation safer encompassed all three.

CAPTAIN RALPH S. JOHNSON

CAPTAIN RALPH S. JOHNSON WITH
CAPTAIN BILLY WALKER, JR

As a young army cadet he was one of only four to successfully complete the rigorous training and wash-out program the air corps had at that time. Following his training, Johnson so impressed his superiors that he, a mere lieutenant, was chosen to be the personal pilot for General Wynans. He flew the General around the country in the tri-motored Fokker F-3, the army's most advanced transport at that time.

Ralph would wave off any suggestion of his having superior abilities by saying he was just in the right place at the right time. Those of us fortunate enough to have known Ralph, and to have worked with him, know that it is more a case of his having "The Right Stuff". Time and again he would come up with a simple solution to a problem. My father called him "a pilot's pilot" and, as a youngster, I marveled at his innate ability to get things out of airplanes that designers didn't believe was possible.

After having flown with many of the old pre-United NAT pilots in the Ford Tri-Motors, Ralph ended up in Cheyenne flying everything United had, the old 40B, 247's, DC-3's, and DC-4's. During the war he flew hundreds of B-17's, B-24's, C-87's, and PBY's as they came through the modification center. He flew the Pacific too, as a command pilot, delivering war material via United's Pacific operations.

It becomes easy to see how the Cheyenne airport became rich with history. We need only to know about the men and women who breathed life into this airport that was so much a center of aviation activity for half a century.

Ralph Johnson, more than any other, personifies the phenomenal growth and development of aviation at Cheyenne. Sure others, like my father, Slim Lewis and General Phillips, made significant contributions. However, no other individual can top all that Johnson did to improve performance, efficiency and above all, safety.

Johnson's "All Weather Flight Methods" with his patented "Stabilized Approach" was conceived in the late 30s. He developed, tested and proved the concept with the 1941 production of a film showing the tremendous benefits of utilizing this technique. This innovation alone would qualify Johnson for great honors as it has saved countless lives and will save countless more in the future. It is the standard for all pilots (military-airline-general-aviation) in approach-landing procedures then and now. Modern swept-winged jets could not safely operate using any other technique.

The list of the Johnson legacies is a long one—propeller and wing de-icing systems, fuel distribution systems, cockpit resource management techniques and the "coordinator" check list, to name a few.

Douglas aircraft "borrowed" Johnson from United so that he could help resolve some engineering problems with the DC-3. He test flew and delivered many to various airlines. He was the primary test pilot for the DC-5, a wonderful airplane that succumbed to internal politics at Douglas.

Now in his 90th year, ol' Ralph can look back with tremendous pride in his accomplishments. But he won't! If you catch him sitting around, he is thinking of something that will improve things. But if he would reminisce, he could look back at being one of those rare airmen still flying at over age 80, who really would leave this world better than he found it. Most, if not all, Flying octogenarians fly small pleasure aircraft. Not Ralph! He flew converted WWII bombers across the tops of sagebrush combating fire ants and forest fires until a few short years ago. Just a few months ago, he flew the A-320 swept-winged jet transport in America West's fifteen million dollar full-flight simulator.

When he wasn't flying airplanes, he was modifying them for improved efficiency. He developed new techniques and invented a wing-tip dispensing system and a host of other improvements for agriculture aircraft.

Along with all this, Johnson was an entrepreneur and, for a while, an elected state representative. He helped start Teton National Insurance Company, operated several aviation enterprises and was president of Ideal

Aerosmith. He operated two other airports, one in Douglas, Arizona, the other in Banbridge, Georgia. He had help too—and she sits over there. Stand up, Ruth, so everyone can see just why ol' Ralph was so successful.

Just prior to WWII, there was a growing need to train the pilots for the airplanes that the government was producing to defend democracy against the tyranny of Germany, Italy, and Japan. Plains Airways was formed, and by wars end they had trained several thousand pilots and mechanics for the Army Air Corps. Over fourteen million gallons of gasoline were pumped into transient army aircraft by Plains Petroleum, a subsidiary of Plains Airways.

The main base of operations was at Cheyenne's airport with bases at Laramie and Ft. Morgan, Colorado (a pre-glider school run by Marv Stevenson, the former Wyoming State Aeronautics Director). Additionally, there were several instructor's with aircraft stationed at various airports around the state.

Plains became a major employer and contributor to the Cheyenne economy. In my early airline career, I flew with several Frontier captains who had been trained by Plains Airways. Some were personally trained by my father, Pic Walker. The late General Sam Phillips, one of our inductees tonight, was trained at Plain's Laramie base.

My father was a key to the success of Plains Airways. The University of Wyoming designated him "Professor of Aeronautics". He was in charge of the daily flight operations and was a pioneer charter member of the Civil Air Patrol. A few years ago he was honored by the CAP and National Aeronautic Association for his contributions to aviation. In fact, he was the sole surviving charter member of the original CAP wing commanders. He was invited by Fiorello LaGuardia, mayor of New York City, and Gill Robb Wilson, a well-known aviation writer, to help with the formation of the CAP in 1940-41. My Dad became Wyoming's first Wing Commander. Red Kelso, the one largely responsible for the formation of Wyoming's Aviation Hall of Fame, recently retired as Wyoming's Wing Commander.

After the war, Pic Walker and Ralph Johnson started Plains Aerial Survey's using a DC-3 and a special geological apparatus. They discovered the vast oil aquifer that lays between Cheyenne and Denver.

MAJOR W. DILLARD "PIC" WALKER

My father was involved in aerial agriculture work using a large aircraft just after WWII. He also sold refurbished aircraft, and interestingly, sold three DC-3's to Barry Goldwater for Arizona Airways which soon after became Frontier. So, these three DC-3's were among the aircraft I flew when I first went to work at Frontier. However, I didn't find out that they had been my father's until a few weeks before he died. He, as with the rest of the men we are honoring tonight, was a doer, not a talker. He never said much, but when he spoke it usually meant something.

About 1950, he moved his family to Saratoga, where he became involved in ranching and developing the Saratoga Inn, where he, almost single-handedly, built the beautiful golf course there—the first all-grass golf course in the state.

During this time, he still flew. He used a Luscombe T8F and later, a Cessna 180 to try and control the Platte River mosquito. He and Don Donelan modernized Shively Field so the larger corporate aircraft could fly into Saratoga's airport. He installed runway lights and lengthened the runway using his old Caterpillar road grader. He taught Jerry Donelan and me to fly there with Donelan being his last student as I finished up with Les Larson over here in Cheyenne.

GENERAL SAM PHILLIPS

Then in 1958, he moved our family to Arizona where he entered the real estate business with former Cheyomingite, Tilton Kefe. He used aircraft for several years in conjunction with his real estate work, finally retiring in the mid '70s. He flew west March 31, 1992, after putting up the good fight.

After having been invited to give this evening's address, I called Mrs. Phillips to find out a few things about her husband. It was then I discovered that her husband had learned to fly in my father's flight school.

We could spend the whole evening, and then some on General Phillips' biography. He did it all, and well. Although born in Springerville, Arizona, he grew up in Cheyenne and graduated from the University of Wyoming in 1942 where he learned to fly at Plains Airways. During the war he was a P-38 and P-51 fighter pilot earning more than a dozen decorations.

After the war, he completed his masters degree in electrical engineering and became involved with research and development of advanced aircraft and missile systems. He was the author of the agreement with Great Britain over the use of IRBM missiles. This earned him the Legion of Merit.

In 1964 he was assigned to NASA as Director of the Appollo Manned Lunar Landing Program and, later, was Director of the Space and Missile Systems Organization (SAMSO). In 1970, he became Director of The National Security Agency and was Commander of the Air Force Systems Command.

He was awarded two NASA distinguished service Medals for his part in getting men to the moon. The Smithsonian awarded him the Langley Medal as the 14th person so honored since 1909 when it was first awarded to the Wright Brothers. He received an honorary Doctor of Laws degree from the University of Wyoming. He was awarded the White U.S.A.F. Space Trophy and was elected to the National Academy of Engineering. His widow, the former Betty Anne Brown also hails from Cheyenne. It is so nice to meet you, Betty, and to have you here for this great event.

If all this seems like a lot, you should read Sam's biography. He, and the three men who brought us here tonight make you proud to be from Cheyenne. I am tired of hearing about athletes being our role models; the men and women, too, like Sam, Ralph, Slim and my Dad are the real role models for our youth.

So, what is happening with the Cheyenne airport these days? One would suppose this old airport's spirit to be kind of lonesome for all the hustle and bustle it has seen over these past 75 years. However, the spirit is still very much alive with general aviation activity, the Air Guard, Civil Air Patrol and one commuter airline still coaxing air travelers aboard for a short hop to Denver. But it will never be like it was when Slim, Ralph, Pic & Sam witnessed its zenith. From the days of buffalo roaming freely to men in space, this ol' town has kept pace and still retained its special karma. For the past 75 years this ol' airport has been a special part of that. I'm betting that it will be here for another 75 and Ralph just might too!

Even for me, a "Johnnie-Come-Lately", I have some wonderful recollections. Seeing the airport again after all these years caused me to reflect back when I was learning to fly here and, later, working for Lou Dominico selling (or, rather, hoping to sell) some airplanes. Still, for me, the best of times was flying for Frontier Airlines which, incidentally, flew through Cheyenne for more than forty years and for half of that time it was my pleasure. I miss those days.

Did you know that, at the time of its demise in 1986, Frontier was the safest airline in the world-wide history of civil aviation? The measure of that record is by the most stringent means, that of the number of take-offs and landings. I doubt it will be equaled as Frontier flew in and out of black holes and mountain valleys, day and night, and in the worst of weather in those old DC-3's and Convairs—SAFELY. She flew from coast to coast and from Canada down to Old Mexico—SAFELY. Sadly, having a safe record wasn't enough to save Frontier.

Frontier lost but one revenue passenger when a DC-3 lost a battle to low level icing in a storm near Miles City, Montana, over 30 years ago. Sure, Frontier lost a few bags now and then, but the passengers made it to their destinations, SAFELY. Also, Frontier never had a second's disruption to its schedule due to employee unrest. Now that one, is a rare piece of airline trivia. It was greed and pernicious owners along with invidious management that did her in.

In closing, I would offer that if any of you have a fear of flying—YOU SHOULDN'T. We never have had one of those things stay up there yet!

I appreciate the hospitality, and it IS NICE to be back home.

Thank you.